How Can I Help?

*What You Can (And Can't) Do To Counsel
A Friend, Colleague Or Family Member With
A Problem*

Anna Ranieri PhD
&
Joe Gurkoff MA

PRAISE FOR *HOW CAN I HELP?*

"In this useful and accessible book, Anna and Joe extract from their extensive counseling backgrounds the therapeutic essence that will enable anyone to be of help to someone they care about. They show the reader how to be helpful – which centers on listening and empathizing-- or to choose skillfully when not to engage. With common sense and kindness, they show us how we can and cannot be of help."

Fred Luskin, PhD, author of *Forgive for Good* and *Stress Free for Good*

"A thoughtful, insightful book that can make you a better friend, parent, or colleague. Highly recommended."

Janice Kaplan, bestselling author and former Editor-in-Chief, *Parade*

"*HOW CAN I HELP?* is a thoughtful and practical primer to guide the well-intentioned helper. This wonderful new book covers all the bases, taking you from start to finish.

You'll be glad you read it-and the person you helped even more so!"

Roderick M. Kramer, PhD, William R. Kimball Professor of Organizational Behavior Graduate School of Business, Stanford University

"When is the last time you put down the phone or walked away from a friend, family member or colleague wishing you could have helped them more effectively? Anna and Jose use their years of counseling experience to guide you in deciding when and how to help. They even coach you through the exit process so you can return to your original relationship. You will find many ways to use the insights they provide."

Julia Schlam Edelman, M.D., FACOG, NCMP Author, Menopause Matters: Your Guide to a Long and Healthy Life; and *The Harvard Medical School Guide to Successful Sleeping Strategies for Women*

How Can I Help?

What You Can (and Can't) Do
to Counsel a Friend, Colleague
or Family Member With a Problem

Trousdale Press

Anna Ranieri PhD & Joe Gurkoff MA

First Edition

ISBN-10-0692304320

ISBN-13-9780692304327

To Helpers Everywhere

Contents

Preface

Why should you read this book?

If we could talk with you right now, we hope that you'd say something like:

"I'm reading this book because I'd like to know how to help a friend who's going through a hard time."

OR

"I picked up this book so that I can respond to a colleague who has some conflict with her boss."

OR

"I'd like to know what to do about my cousin, who keeps telling me that he wants to get into shape, but can never find time to exercise."

If you're saying *something* like this, we think that this book will be useful to you. We wrote it to give you the information you need to help a family member, colleague or friend who seems to have a problem. We'll give you an overview of the helping process as well as a how-to guide for each step of the way.

This book won't teach you how to be a psychotherapist. It will, we think, help you gain some confidence and competence in listening and responding to someone as they describe one of those challenging situations that come up for anyone and everyone from time to time.

Why did we write this book?

We - Anna and Joe - met when we were both master's students in counseling psychology, working as interns at a crisis center and preparing to become psychotherapists. Anna had worked in corporate marketing and in university fundraising. Joe had been a financial advisor and stockbroker.

At the crisis center, we started by "working the phones" on those late night shifts when people call in with large or small problems, and in various states of distress or frustration. Later, we became counseling interns, meeting face-to-face with clients who came to the crisis center for counseling. Some of these people were in really tough situations. With close clinical supervision, we had the opportunity to practice the theories we learned in graduate school, and try to help our clients solve their problems.

We've kept in touch for twenty years, and one day over lunch Anna told Joe that she thought a book called something like "How Can I Help?" would be worth writing. In it, the helping skills that therapists use could be distilled for the lay person who just wants to help a friend, colleague, or family member. Anna had observed that very intelligent and well-meaning people often do a poor job of listening to and empathizing with a friend who had a problem. They didn't realize that a helping conversation is different from a standard conversation. Rather than listening all the way through, they offered advice and "fixes" too quickly. They never allowed the person to fully explain and begin to get to the root of the problem.

Joe liked the idea of "How Can I Help?" and quickly discovered that there were no other books on the market that took exactly this approach. When Anna and Joe polled people they knew, and asked whether they would be interested in this idea, they learned that many would welcome some assistance in becoming a better helper. And so this book was born.

Introduction

You Can Help By...

Listening

In this chapter you'll learn (or, if you've studied listening techniques before, you'll be reminded) that listening in itself can be a very powerful way to help, and is a gift we don't always give. But sometimes, listening alone won't get you far enough in understanding exactly what your friend is troubled by. So we share with you some ways to harness the power of:

Clarifying The Issues & Defining The Problem

Your coworker may be experiencing a whole universe of annoyances and difficulties, each one of them a potential candidate to work on. Here's where those goofy questions that therapists and other helpers ask can be useful to you, too. In this chapter, we'll show you how they help you to learn more and to zero in on what's most important to him at this time so that you can end up discussing the same problem, not two different ones. Once you've defined the problem, you can help by:

Setting The Goal

Sure, there are lots of ways for your niece to address the problem as you've identified it. But which goal is desirable, feasible and right for her? You can help her to consider which alternative is best. But if you don't see her *doing* anything, you can help by:

Confronting

Many of us will say that we don't like confrontation. Who does?! But if, despite your efforts to listen, help him define the issues and explore ways to address them, your son continues to deny that he has a problem, then confronting him becomes the best way to help. We'll show you how to confront someone you care about in a way that's palatable for you and that works. OK, now they're on board and you can help by:

Making A Plan

The problem your coworker has may have existed for a long time or it may have arisen last week. In either case, she has to make something change in order to solve the problem she's experiencing. To make a fully effective change, she has to start with a plan. You can't execute the plan for her, but you can help her create one that she can follow. And you can help by:

Keeping On Track

The best laid plans sometimes go awry. You can help your friend by encouraging him to follow his plan, bounce back from setbacks, and appreciate his small steps forward. But sometimes you can help by:

Finding Professional Helpers

We emphasize all through this book that you're not a professional helper. There are times when a professional is needed. You may want to help your friend, colleague or family member to find the professional resources he needs to work out the solution to his problem. In this chapter, we'll remind you that this is particularly important when certain kinds of complex issues are involved.

Leaving The Helping Role

When you've done what you can to help, the next step is to leave the helping role and resume your prior relationship. We'll show you how to do it gracefully.

Author's Notes

There are thousands of problems that a friend could have. While we can't address every one of them in this book, we've chosen examples that can apply to many common situations, such as problems at work, in relationships, family, and health. Rather than create a comprehensive guide to solving one particular kind of problem, our focus is on the process of helping people to solve their problems, whatever they may be.

As we describe each step in the helping process, we'll tell you what it is, why it works, how to do it, and how to know if it's worked. We've presented examples that are basic and concise, in language that is simple and straightforward. Our goal is not to write a dramatic masterpiece; it is to give you a practical format you can build on using your own style and words.

We've designed the book to be read from start to finish or to be started anywhere in between. You may choose to quit reading at any point in the book. You may choose to disengage at any point in the helping process. We'll keep mentioning that. We'll keep reminding you of what you can do, what you can't do, and what you can choose to do - or not.

For simplicity's sake, we'll use the word friend to stand for whomever it is you're helping: a family member, friend or colleague. Chapter by chapter, we'll alternate our use of the feminine or masculine pronoun.

Chapter One

The Nature Of Helping

The Nature Of Helping

This chapter is about the difference between what people think helping is and what really helps. It's about what works and what doesn't.

Some people think of helping as:

- Taking over
- Giving advice
- Lending money
- Saying "There, there."

Any one of these could be truly helpful, but the odds of them working are discouragingly low if that's how you start. Leave any preconceived notions behind as you read this book, and we'll show you what really works and when it can be most effective.

Take, for example, the difference between helping and giving advice. You can give all the advice you want, but be aware that the only time it helps is when it's asked for.

We've found that there are three basic requirements for helping someone with a problem. You'll need:

1. The genuine desire to help and the genuine desire of another to be helped.
2. A relationship with the person who has the problem. Your relationship doesn't have to be a life-long friendship. It does have to have a basis for trust and confidence.
3. Time. Do you have the time to work all the way through the problem? Or do you only have time to play a part in getting your friend closer to a solution for his or her problem?

If these requirements are not fulfilled, you may choose to refer the person to a professional helper (see Chapter 8: Helping Them Find Professional Helpers). If, at any later time, these three basic requirements are no longer fulfilled, you can choose to disengage (see Chapter 9: Leaving the Helping Role).

Let's look at the way desire, relationship and time come into play in several different helping situations.

The Crisis Hotline

George has a problem and calls the hotline to seek help. He reaches a volunteer whom he's never met (and never will). The volunteer may be in another city or even another state. Here we have someone who knows he has a problem and knows he wants or needs to do something about it. At the other end of the line is a person who has enough of a desire to help that he's undergone training and committed several hours a week to helping troubled callers.

Desire ✓

George and the volunteer have a temporary relationship. It lasts for the length of the call, which might be 15 minutes, or an hour, or more. George trusts the volunteer to listen, keep George's identity anonymous, and help to the best of her ability. George has no need to be embarrassed or ashamed. He can hang up at any time. He has confidence that the volunteer is trained to help and will attempt to use her best judgment in aiding him.

Relationship ✓

The volunteer, by the same token, knows that George has reached her because he has a real problem. She knows that her time helping him will be well spent because George is ready to work though the problem. The volunteer's time is limited, but she is willing to spend as much of it as she has with George. So, now is the time. The problem has immediacy for George and he wants help right now. The volunteer answers the phone ready to help.

Time ✓

The Professional Counselor

Martha has a problem and she makes an appointment with a career counselor, executive coach or psychotherapist. Her desire to be helped has prompted her to take the time and make the effort (not to mention paying the bill) to address her problem. The professional counselor wants to help: he's in the business of helping people.

Desire ✓

The relationship might begin when Martha first calls the counselor, or in their first meeting. It grows over the time that they work together. There's an explicit or implicit contract for the counselor to provide the help that Martha wants. Martha will actively use the counselor's help as they work toward a solution of her problem.

Relationship ✓

Martha calls this particular counselor because she knows he has experience solving problems like hers. His reputation gives her the confidence that he has the specific skills and training to help her find solutions. She believes that the counselor is trustworthy, that he will maintain confidentiality in all their meetings, and will keep her best interests in mind at all times.

A word about confidentiality

It is the practice of professional counselors to keep confidential everything that their clients tell them. There are certain circumstances, however, when the counselor is required to break this confidentiality. If a client reveals that he is planning to hurt himself or someone else, or that a child or elder has been abused, then the counselor may be required by law to alert the appropriate authorities. Rules about confidentiality should be discussed in the first meeting. If they're not, the client can ask what the counselor's policy is about confidentiality.

The counselor trusts that Martha intends to use his help. He and Martha both understand that their relationship exists for the purpose of solving the problem. It's a professional relationship, not a personal one. Martha doesn't have to concern herself with taking care of the therapist in their meetings, and the counselor doesn't have to worry about taking care of Martha outside of their meetings. This limitation is one of the keys to making the process work.

The time involved in this helping process may be a matter of weeks, months, or years. The process lasts as long as both Martha and the counselor feel that their meetings serve her purpose.

The time together ends either when Martha and the counselor feel that the problem has been solved, or when the counselor feels that he can go no further in helping Martha with her problem.

Time ✓

The Old Friend

Your old friend Frank approaches you and tells you he has a problem. This is what friends do. It's a characteristic of friendship that friends talk about their problems with each other. So, it's clear that he wants some help, and probably clear that you want to help him.

Desire ✓

You and Frank already have an ongoing relationship, and the trust and the confidence in the helping process come from the fact that you've been down this road before. If you haven't, he knows that you care enough about his well-being to do your best to help. He trusts that you won't have a hidden agenda or ulterior motive, so he has the confidence to come to you.

Relationship ✓

You may want to give Frank as much time as it takes to help, and on some days, that's possible. On other days, your job, family, or other obligations may limit the time that you have to help.

When Frank turns to you with a problem, he understands that you may not have the time to help him find an ultimate solution on the spot. What he might have in mind is a series of walks, lunches or phone conversations to help him over time. Or Frank may just want a single idea that you can supply in a relatively short conversation.

Time ✓

Another word about confidentiality

Some people share everything with their spouses, and some people don't. So don't be surprised if Frank wants you to assure him that you won't repeat what he says to anyone, including your spouse, your brother or a mutual friend.

Occupational Hazards and other Gray Areas

Let's look at a couple of instances in which the desire, relationship or time to help may be unclear.

The seatmate on the plane or the train

You've just opened your book or computer when the person next to you introduces himself and before you know it he's launched into the recital of a problem that he's having with his wife. You don't have the desire to help; you don't have a relationship with him, professional or personal; and you were looking forward to getting some work done. On the other hand, you might decide that you want to help anyway. In this case, the desire to help is there, the relationship is the anonymous connection that two fellow travelers have, and the time available is dictated by your estimated time of arrival.

The client in your shop or business

You practice as a hairdresser, massage therapist or financial planner. Sometimes people tell you things that they wouldn't tell their partners, colleagues or therapists. Here again, you may or may not have the desire, or feel that you have the appropriate relationship or the time to help. But you worry that not helping may result in losing a client. You might want to acknowledge their distress, but tell them that you're not equipped to help them with this type of problem and encourage them to seek professional help.

The person you manage

You're a manager in your organization, and a man who reports to you tells you that a family problem may be affecting his performance. In this case, you might have a personal desire to help, or feel that it's your responsibility as a manager to make sure that his job gets done. But here, your relationship with the individual is a professional one based on the objectives of your team, and your time is constrained by the pace of the workplace and your other duties. You can express your desire to help but acknowledge that at work your main responsibility is to manage him and the rest of the team. If the problem is urgent, you can help by suggesting that he call a hotline, or by referring him to an employee assistance program or a professional counselor outside of the workplace.

A final word about confidentiality

It's a good policy to be discreet when someone approaches you in a work environment. When someone talks with you in a non-professional setting, the decision about confidentiality is up to you.

If you've gotten this far, and you still want to help....

We assume that you're not the volunteer on a crisis line and you're not a professional therapist, but you are a family member, friend or co-worker. Let's say that you want to help, feel that the relationship is appropriate for helping, and are willing to put in the time.

So, you can help by.....**Listening**

Chapter Two

Listening

Listening

Take a moment to think of someone you've especially enjoyed talking to; perhaps a parent or a grandparent, a teacher, a friend or your first love. Can you remember how exciting it was to be sharing something of yourself with them that you couldn't share with anyone else? Do you remember the warmth you felt for the person who gave you all the time and encouragement you needed to tell them what was on your mind and in your heart?

Now think of someone who *didn't* listen. Someone who was too busy, who didn't seem to "get it", who teased you about the hopes, fears, joys or sorrows you tried to share. Remember how bad you felt when you realized that they hadn't cared to listen when you wanted to talk about something that meant a great deal to you?

In this chapter, we will show you how important listening is, how it works and how to do it. We can't guarantee that you'll be an ideal listener right away. We do believe that, once you understand the basics of listening, you'll feel confident that you can make a big difference to a friend with a problem. All you need is a genuine desire to give it a go.

You Can Help By Listening

Helping begins with listening. It's the first and most critical step. If you don't listen, it's unlikely you'll be able to be helpful, no matter what you do.

At this point, some of you might be thinking, "Wait a minute! You're telling me something I already know. I'm already a good listener. Why else would people talk to me about their problems? Are you saying I haven't been helpful?"

What we're saying to those of you who have listening skills is that it can't hurt to revisit the basics, fine tune the skills you have and maybe learn new skills so that, next time someone turns to you, you can be even more effective.

Others might be thinking, "Hold on there! I've shared my problems with people before. They've listened to what I said, but they weren't helpful at all. Are you saying that learning about listening is going to make me more effective than people who've tried to help me in the past?"

In a word, yes. We're going to show you how it's done so you can be an effective helper.

This raises the question:

What Is Listening?

The answer is: it depends on the context - that is, what we're listening to and what we're listening for. We listen differently depending on whether we are:

- Taking a hearing test
- Listening for the phone to ring
- Following the sound of the wind in the trees
- Tuning in to the evening news
- Getting the scoop on an eccentric neighbor
- Hearing out a friend with a problem

As you can see, there is more than one way to listen. Before we get into a more detailed explanation of "listening to help," we want to talk about everyday, conversational listening. It's important for you to be able to tell one from the other, so that you can see how "listening to help" works when other kinds of listening don't.

Conversational Listening

Conversation is an informal, unstructured exchange of information between two people. It can also be a creative, playful form of recreation that's a lot of fun. For some people there's nothing better than having a good conversation with a friend.

Is it any wonder that the most popular TV shows are about conversations? *Seinfeld* is a well loved, long -running example. Every episode has at least one 'sitting around, talking' segment. When Jerry, George & Elaine are sitting together in their local restaurant, talking over their cups of coffee, millions of viewers feel they're in on the conversation.

Unfortunately, a free-flowing, no-holds-barred approach we enjoy with colleagues, friends and relations isn't appropriate when we are addressing a problem. In fact, in this context, the casual approach can be counter-productive.

Listening to Help

When you're listening to help, you have a goal. This is a basic and essential difference between what you do in casual conversation and what you do when listening to help.

Your goal in listening to help is to gain an understanding of the whole picture so that you can put the problem into perspective. Your success in reaching this objective depends on your openness to hear without judgment what the other person has to say.

It's what your friend says that matters; what you think about it does not.

The whole picture has two components: objective and subjective.

- The objective involves the facts and the details of the situation.
- The subjective relates to your friend's thoughts and feelings; that is, what the situation means to your friend.

This means you need facts and details. But if you or your friend wants to go further, you need more than just the facts and details. You also need to know how your friend interprets them and, possibly, how he feels about them.

We know, this sounds like a lot to accomplish. Not to worry. We're going to show you how to do it.

In the following examples, you'll see what listening to help is and how it differs from what you do in a casual conversation.

Example

Your friend says "I had a really high cholesterol reading on my last blood test."

At this point in a casual conversation, you might:

- Ask a question - "Who's your doctor?"
- Make a comment – "Nobody likes going to the doctor."
- Chime in with as story - "Yeah, I got some bad news today too."
- Make suggestions - "You should always go to the doctor in the morning, when your cholesterol is lower."

In contrast, listening to help is much more like an interview than a dialogue. When you're listening to help, you put your personal comments and questions on hold. You focus entirely on your friend: what he's saying, what he's trying to say, what he hasn't thought to say, what he thinks, how he feels, how he'd like to feel. Your curiosity should be directed toward finding out as much as you can about what he's saying and feeling. You'll be surprised at how much effort it takes to hold that focus when you try to listen *this* carefully. How do you do this?

Example

You might ask a question to elicit the objective facts:
   "Is your cholesterol a lot higher than it was before?"

He might say in response:
   "Yes, it's gone up 30 points in just one year."

You can ask a question to elicit his subjective feelings about this:
   "How did you react to the results?"

He might say in response:
   "I've been pretty worried and scared about this."
Now it's time to keep asking questions so that you can understand where the feelings come from:
   "What are you afraid could happen?"

This might lead you to the underlying meaning:
> *"My father died of a heart attack when he was only 52 and I'm afraid that I could die early too, leaving my wife and kids without anyone to take care of them."*

Notice that, by continuing to ask those questions, you've gone all the way from a simple statement that your friend made about his cholesterol reading to the objective facts, the subjective feelings, and the personal meaning of this event for him at this point in his life. It took a while to get there, but you can see the value of getting the whole picture.

This process is often called 'active listening'. It's a concept that's been around for quite a while. We're not sure who coined the term or where it comes from, but it's widely used in articles, books and classes about enhancing interpersonal communications. Perhaps you've come across one of these "How to Listen So Your Employee, Daughter, Son, Husband or Wife Feels Heard" books or seminars somewhere along the way.

Listening to help incorporates active listening and uses it as a foundation for a more complete helping process. You'll see that process in action throughout this book.

Remember how we told you, in The Nature of Helping, that three elements are necessary for the process to work: desire, relationship and time? In listening to help, you're using those three elements to be successful. In listening, you're demonstrating the desire to help as your friend has demonstrated the desire to be heard. You're using your relationship, and deepening it, as you work to understand a problem. And you're taking time, quite a bit of time, in order to fully hear the problem in a way that conversational listening doesn't allow. These three elements give 'listening to help' a good foundation for success.

Why Does Listening Help?

Listening helps because it encourages your friend to put his thoughts into words. When he believes that you're listening, he'll think more deeply about his dilemma so he can explain it for your benefit. He might only become aware of what he's thinking when he has the time to speak his thoughts out loud. This allows him to see his situation in a way that he never has before. And that's not all: The more thoroughly he develops his thoughts, the more your friend will have access to the feelings he has about them. So by listening, you've helped him further his own understanding.

Psychotherapists know that clients can experience a deep emotional benefit from expressing their thoughts and feelings out loud to another person. In the real world, this is what people mean when they say "It really felt good to get that off my chest". Whether "that" is anger, sorrow, fear or doubt, people feel liberated when they've expressed it out loud.

Your friend wants someone to invite him to express his thoughts and feelings, someone who cares, someone who will listen without judging. Once he has spoken his thoughts and feelings, and seen that the world hasn't ended as a result of his revealing them, he may experience a great sense of relief.

Not all problems require dramatic solutions. Don't be surprised if it turns out that being heard is all your friend needs.

Never underestimate the power of listening or the effect of being heard.

How To Do It - Part 1

Picture this....

The phone rings. You pick it up and a friend says, "I can't take it any more!"

Does this mean that he's angry with his wife, fed up by his kids, overwhelmed by his parents or about to quit his job?

A statement like this is hard to understand and easy to misinterpret until you've got a grasp of the whole picture. In listening to help, the context is the whole picture. You need the objective facts and the subjective feelings.

Let's put this question on hold for the time being and start with a more general example to give you an idea of how to do it.

Example 1

Your friend is experiencing a problem that you want to understand. In listening to help, you have a specific goal: gain an understanding of the whole picture so that you can put your friend's problem into perspective.

With your focus fixed on what he says, you listen to all the facts. Then you attempt to paraphrase the facts ("I think you said…") and ask him if you've heard them correctly. You keep trying until he is satisfied that you have the facts right.

Then you ask him to tell you what the facts mean to him. In your own words, you restate the meaning and ask if you've understood correctly. You keep at it until he's satisfied that you understand what the facts mean to him. Be prepared for your, or his, impatience or discomfort. It's not always easy to probe for facts and meaning, but it's the only way that you can begin to hear and to help him.

To be effective, you have to keep the focus entirely on him. You'll have to resist the urge to interject your own thoughts and feelings. This is, of course, easier said than done. As we've said, it takes practice to feel comfortable with this kind of listening.

Example 2

OK, now back to a more specific example: The phone rings, and your friend says, " I can't take it any more."

By listening to help, you can generate the whole picture from a very limited statement, like this one. It's a joint venture, a shared inquiry that begins with the facts you already know, and progresses with a series of questions and restatements to bring out the critical issues and let you develop a clear understanding of the big picture. You:

Listening

1. Ask questions to learn the facts:

   a. "What's been happening?"
   b. "Is this something new or different?"
   c. "Is it getting worse?"

2. Put the facts into the proper context:

   a. "How did it start?"
   b. "Who does it involve?"
   c. "What have you done so far?"

3. Identify your friend's emotional response to the situation

   a. "How do you feel about it?"
   b. "How bad is it?"
   c. "Are you more angry than sad?"

4. Understand the meaning of that response:

   a. "What does it mean to you?"
   b. "What's at stake?"
   c. "What are you afraid might happen?"
   d. "What are you hoping might happen?"

5. Summarize what you've heard:

    a.   "Let me make sure I understand: do you mean...?"
    b.   "So it sounds like you're saying..."

6. Confirm that you got it right:

    a.   "Did I get that right?"
    b.   "Is that what you were trying to tell me?"
    c.   "Is there anything I missed?"

You'll notice that most of the questions in our examples are open-ended: each one requires more than a yes or no answer. *Open-ended questions* like these will keep the other person talking and will get you more information.

In fact, it might help to think of *listening to help* as an interview that a newspaper reporter would conduct to gather and organize information in order to give a reader an accurate presentation of relevant facts and details. Like the newspaper reporter, you want to be asking lots of questions. But one question that can be very tricky is the question that starts with "why". We recommend that you avoid the "why" question if you possibly can.

Example 3

Consider these two pairs of questions:

1) A. "Why do you let your husband treat you that way?"
Versus
1) B. "How do you feel when your husband treats you like that?"

2) A. "Why do you stay?"
Versus
2) B. "What keeps you there?"

As you were reading the "A" questions, did you feel that they might make someone become defensive? As you were reading the "B" questions, did you feel that they were less judgmental?

Which question in each pair would be easier for you to answer? Which would help you to reveal more about your situation?

'Why' questions can be the hardest to answer. They can sound judgmental or psychologically invasive. Your friend may become reluctant to talk if he feels vulnerable to judgment, psychoanalyzing, rejection or ridicule. A better strategy is to get information by using a who, what, when, where or how question.

When listening to help, it's crucial that you withhold any critical, editorial and advisory comments that come to mind.

How To Do It - Part 2

Listening to help is *not* what we do most of the time, and it takes practice to do it well.

You can practice in a casual conversation. Try pausing for five seconds after your friend finishes what he's saying. Don't respond, don't push on to the next disclosure. When you're comfortable doing this, try pausing for ten seconds. By doing this, you give him a chance to add to or revise what he's said.

You can practice keeping the focus on a friend, too. When talking with someone who says, "What do you think about my getting a tattoo?", it's very tempting to jump right in with your opinion. You can practice keeping the focus on the other person by saying, "We can talk about what I think later. Now I'd like to hear what you think, so that I make sure I get what you're saying." Even with an issue as seemingly cosmetic as this, you may be surprised at how much your friend appreciates getting his point across first.

Listen for the feelings that go with the facts. You can practice identifying feelings by using this list of seven emotions:

1. **Happiness**
2. **Sadness**
3. **Desire**
4. **Anger**
5. **Love**
6. **Hatred**
7. **Fear**

Example 4

Practice by naming the emotion that you think a friend is expressing, and ask if your friend is feeling that emotion:

"Sounds like you're angry about that."

See if your friend says, "that's right," or if he corrects you by naming another emotion.

If you're worried that a friend will think there's something wrong when you pause, or throw a question back at him, or ask about his feelings, you needn't be. He probably won't even have noticed. He's more likely just to enjoy the opportunity to keep talking and the chance to say more. Later, though, he might think about how lucky he is that you're such a good listener.

If all this sounds painstakingly time consuming, you've got the idea. Listening to help is a skill that's easier for some to learn than others, but it takes conscious effort in any case. We all have difficulty putting our personal comments and questions on hold while listening to help.

It's worth repeating: *This effort is worth your while.* You'll find this approach to be much more productive and satisfying than trying to wedge your point of view into the dialogue and getting yourself into an argument over whose point of view is the right one. In the long run, however, this approach to listening actually saves time. It assures that you'll find out what the real problem is before you go down the wrong path.

If, at this point, this kind of effort is more than you want to make, you can decide not to be the helper. You can refer your friend to a professional helper (see Chapter 8) or leave the helping role (see Chapter 9).

Example 5

Your colleague says his supervisor is dissatisfied with his work and he's worried about losing his job.

Responses like: "Sounds like your boss is a jerk", or "that's not fair", or "here's what I'd do," seem to show that you're on your friend's side, but the real effect of these responses is to draw the focus away from fact-finding. In using them, you risk missing out on important information.

It's much better to say, "Tell me more." Whatever he says next will bring you both another step closer to understanding his situation.

What if, when you ask more questions, you begin to get the impression that your friend's take on the situation is implausible? That's OK. Your goal at this point is to understand the big picture from his point of view.

You want to understand his subjective reality, not the objective, verifiable truth. You can listen without agreeing with everything he says because you're offering him *acceptance, not agreement*, and your acceptance can be very powerful.

Saying "unh-hunh" doesn't mean that you agree with him. It simply means that you hear him, you're considering what he's saying, and you're willing to hear more. It means "I'm listening".

How To Do It - Part 3

It's worth withholding your comments until you're sure you have the whole picture. Attempting to intervene or make a judgment now, you risk jumping the gun. If you need to confront your friend at a later stage in the process, you'll have earned the right to do so and will have much more information upon which to base your opinion.

When you're listening to help, your attention is not focused exclusively on words. You're observing body language, tone of voice, and facial expression. These are clues to emotion and meaning.

It's worth mentioning that you're also under observation. Your own body language, tone of voice and facial expression demonstrate your involvement as a listener.

Don't worry about looking and sounding like the stereotypical TV psychotherapist. You know, the one who furrows his brows with concern, says "unh-hunh", nods his head as if to say "I'm with you," then leans forward, looks the client in the eye and says: "And how does that make you feel?"

These kinds of movements and sounds are signals that say: "I'm listening closely and want to know more, so don't worry about me, you can go on as long as you like."

You have your own personal "I'm in no hurry, you have my full attention" facial expressions and body language. Use them; you'll be creating an atmosphere that enables a friend to speak out loud about the complex, difficult thoughts and feelings he's been struggling to deal with.

In a nutshell: Listen, observe, and ask questions. Learn the facts, the details, and what those facts and details mean to your friend. Hear about his real fear or his own personal goal. Take the time to take it all in.

A word about your own emotional responses

As you listen to someone else's story, you may find yourself getting angry or hurt by what they say or how they say it. If you're feeling this way, you're not at that moment in a position to help.

What can you do when your hot buttons get pushed? You'll want to take a break and politely excuse yourself to think through the situation and ask yourself whether you can help this individual under these circumstances.

A word about empathy

Empathy, pity, and sympathy are all natural responses that we have when someone describes a problem. Empathy is the one that plays a role in listening to help. Empathy includes the recognition that another person has a feeling, and an acceptance that he feels that way. You don't have to have experienced the same problem or have had the same feelings in order to demonstrate empathy.

Example

Suppose your friend says: "My doctor tells me that I'm going to need foot surgery. I'm worried that it's really going to hurt and I won't be able to get around for six weeks."

The sympathetic response, "I know how you feel," is open to debate. Let's face it, no one can know exactly how another person feels about anything.

The empathetic response, "I can tell that you're scared and worried," demonstrates that you're not all-knowing, but that you do hear his distress.

Listening has its limits

There are problems that you're not going to be able to help with no matter how well you listen. Take for example a friend who is emotionally or behaviorally out of control. He is creating his own problems, or making his current problems much worse.

Traumatic events, mental illnesses and addictions are possible triggers for out of control behavior. Of these, traumatic events are the easiest to identify and comprehend. In contrast, addictions and mental illnesses can go on for years without being recognized as such – either by the person affected or the ones he affects.

Family members and friends can and do live in the shadow of diseases like alcoholism, anxiety and bi-polar disorders, as well as personality disorders like narcissism and sociopathy, long before realizing their severity and potential danger.

Your friend might not be aware of his own condition. If he is, he might be avoiding treatment. It's quite possible he's not telling you or anyone else the whole story. In any case, without professional training or prior experience, you might spin your wheels for a long time trying to help someone you ultimately can't.

A word about the value of the informed, objective viewpoint of a professional helper

---

When we have plenty of life experience, but we lack specialized training, we can be fooled by what we think we're hearing and seeing. A medical doctor or psychotherapist can quickly recognize that there's more going on beneath the surface.

What do you do if, after going this far, you feel that you're over your head, and that your friend needs professional help? Be honest, but supportive. Say something like "After listening to what you've said, I think this is a really serious problem that's too complicated for the two of us to figure out. I think you need to talk to someone who has more experience with these things than I have." You may be surprised how much your friend appreciates this.

There's more information about finding and referring someone to a professional helper in Chapter 8.

How Do You Know
If Listening Worked?

As we've said, *listening to help* invites people to express their thoughts and feelings and regain a sense of control and self-confidence.

You'll know that listening has worked when your friend says:

"Thank you" *or*

"You're a good listener" *or*

"You've helped me understand" *or*

"I'm lucky to have a friend like you" *or*

"Talking about this has helped. I feel like I've got a handle on it now."

Or if, when you ask if talking about the problem has helped..... he says yes!

It's possible that it has worked but that your effectiveness will not always be acknowledged in words. Sometimes you get visual cues: he seems to be standing taller, looking more relaxed, not gritting his teeth, smiling more. Any of these things that you can observe may mean that you've been successful in really listening.

If people already think of you as a good listener, they might not thank you for what you've done, because they've come to take it for granted. We want to thank you on their behalf, because we recognize the difference that good listening can make in people's lives!

There's another way to measure whether it's worked. And that is, you now know much more about your friend and his state of mind than you did before. Knowing this, you'll feel more comfortable making a decision about continuing to help or not.

Remember, you always have the option to say, "I don't think the two of us can get much further with this. Let's look at what else you could do to get help with this problem."

Sometimes listening is all it takes. Other times, more steps will be required. Several issues may be tangled together so the real essence of the problem isn't yet known.

If listening to help isn't enough, and you want to go further, you can help by....

Clarifying The Issues & Defining The Problem

Chapter Three

Clarifying The Issues &
Defining The Problem

Clarifying The Issues & Defining The Problem

OK, so you've done some listening and even asked some questions to discover how your friend is feeling about the issues she's raised. You've refrained from judging, you've avoided giving advice, and you've steered clear of offering premature solutions. You've kept the focus on her and you've got a lot of information.

The common mistake that people make at this point is to assume that they know enough about the problem to start problem-solving. Don't do it! The risk is that you'll be attempting to solve the wrong problem, and that's an unnecessary risk. You could waste a lot of time and increase your frustration by going off on a tangent that won't be helpful to her in the long run.

Your role now is to help clarify the issues and identify the problem.

What Is Clarifying The Issues & Defining The Problem?

Clarifying the issues and identifying the problem means sorting through the information you've gained by listening. Now, you can pinpoint the problem your friend is actually experiencing.

Just because you have a lot of information and some glimpse of the whole picture doesn't mean that you're ready yet to solve a problem. It may take further digging to identify what the problem really is.

Why Does Clarifying & Defining Help?

In the last chapter, we showed that when you listen, your friend tells you what she's been thinking about her problem.

In reality, however, it's more complicated because people rarely express their thoughts completely, clearly and in logical order. What's more, problems often come bundled together as a confusing tangle of issues. One problem piggybacks on another, and maybe another, and maybe another…

And as if that's not enough, there's that all-too-human tendency to want to get started on solutions with the barest understanding of a problem. Your job now is to take the time your friend needs to chisel away at the issues and decide which is the most critical problem for your friend to solve.

Clarifying the issues and identifying the problem help you isolate the problem from all the other issues revolving around it.

Here's a simple example:

Example 1

What if your friend comes to you and says, "My husband says he wants a divorce."

In casual conversation, it's OK to assume that you understand everything you hear. When trying to help a friend, we suggest you assume that you don't.

In the example above, if you fail to clarify the issues, you might immediately launch into comments about:

- How sad she must feel.
- How disappointed she must be that she's put so much work into her marriage.
- How difficult it is to start over as a single woman.
- Etc., Etc.

The way to make sure that you're not proceeding with false assumptions is to ask questions that will clarify what the issues are and identify the problem your friend wants help with.

If you ask your friend, "How do you feel about the possibility of getting a divorce?"

Now, she may say, "Actually, getting a divorce is a big relief. I'm not worried about my emotional survival. I'm just worried about how we're going to afford two rents!"

Now you know what the real problem is. You can name it and you can identify the practical issues that are the real worry for her.

The process of clarification works because it prevents you from wasting time and effort attacking a superficial problem, while leaving the real problem untouched. It allows you and your friend to solve the problem that's important to her. Once you give the problem a name, you can start to work on the specific issues and get to a solution faster.

How To Do It – Part 1

Let's start with the example of a friend who tells you that she's moving.

Some people look forward to moving; others dread it. So, when your friend announces that she's moving, you need to know more about how she views the situation.

Here are ten common issues people experience when faced with a move:

1. Loss of family relationships and close friendships
2. Loss of connections to doctors, lawyers and other trusted service providers
3. Fear of not being accepted by new neighbors in the new community
4. Anger at having to move
5. Stress over the logistics of moving
6. Organizing the family and helping children with issues of transition

7. Monetary worries
8. Concerns about impact on one's career
9. Loss of existing social network
10. Strain on relationship with spouse or partner

Is leaving her current home a problem for your friend, and, if so, of what type? Is it a practical problem or an emotional problem? Does she fear leaving friends behind, shouldering the expense of moving, having a longer commute to work, being farther away from her aging parents, or just finding a reliable moving company? It's hard to know how the act of moving affects her, so you have to clarify the issues and define the problem from her point of view.

And, to complicate things further, you might LOVE moving and be tempted to assume that she does too. Be sure that you're not confusing your feelings with hers on this issue.

How do you know which of these difficulties your friend is experiencing?

You ask.

A good question to start with is one of the most basic:

"And how is that a problem?"

Moving: Example 1

Your friend says, "My son is really upset about our move because he has to leave his school friends behind."

You ask, "And how is that a problem?"

She says, "I'm going to have to get my son into a new baseball league, my daughter into a theater group, and myself into a new book club."

You say, "OK, do you think the problem is really about starting over?"

If she says, "Yeah, I guess that's what I'm really worried about", then you know that you've identified the problem to help her work on.

But, if she says, "No, that's not it," you have to keep asking simple questions until you can narrow down the possibilities and get to the real problem as she sees it.

Moving: Example 2

Your colleague says, "I finally got elected president of the city council and now I'm being transferred to Baltimore."

You say, "Do you feel guilty about letting people down?"

She says: "No, that's not it. I think what I feel most guilty about is my mother."

You say, "And what happens to your mother when you move?"

She says, "My mother's in a nursing home. Who's going to visit her every Sunday? My sister is mad at me because now she'll be stuck with all the responsibility."

You say, "Would you say that you're more concerned about your lonely mother or your angry sister?"

She may say, "Well, I can handle my sister's anger, but I really feel bad about Mom."

Or she might say, "I know I'll visit Mom eventually, but it's my sister's anger that's hardest for me to take."

As you can see, by asking questions this way, you'll have zeroed in on the problem, you'll be able to name it, and you'll have a better idea of how to proceed with the helping process.

Here's a list of other questions you can ask to help define a problem:

- How bad is it?
- When did it begin?
- What about it makes it a problem for you?
- What's the most pressing issue right now?
- Is there anyone else involved?
- Is money a factor?
- What are you afraid is going to happen?

How To Do It – Part 2

Sometimes, you don't know *what* to ask until you *start* to ask. It's important to begin with general questions like the ones above. Don't worry; as you continue to ask, other questions will come to mind, based upon your friend's answers.

Clarifying the issue by asking this type of question will give you and your friend a better understanding of what's going on. You may come to a point where your friend is stumped. She doesn't have an answer, and possibly doesn't have a clue.

Up until this point, everything you know about the situation has come from her. She's told you what she thinks about the problem, how she feels about it, and what it means to her. Through the other questions that you've asked, you've gained even more information. When she's gone as far as she can go, then you have to jump in to offer your take on what she's said up till now.

This is the first time in the helping process when you can bring something to the table, offer your observations, and provide an objective viewpoint. Remember to leave out the judgment. In the examples below we'll show you how to respond without judging.

Example 3

Your friend says "My son got a speeding ticket and it's been sitting on the hall table for a month. No matter what I say, he won't open it or do anything else about it. I'm at my wit's end. What can I do to make sure he takes care of his ticket?"

Here, the problem your friend describes turns out to be somebody else's problem: her son's. She's not responsible for its solution; he is. You see this, but she doesn't. You might ask:

-Whose problem is this?

-Have you considered that this is more his problem than yours?

If she still doesn't get it, you could say:

"Sounds to me like it's his speeding ticket and his responsibility to deal with it."

She says, "You're right, but if he loses his license, I'll have to drive him around all the time!"

This demonstrates why you go through the whole clarifying process. By asking a series of questions, you get from the general to the specific, and specific problems are easier to solve than general ones. In this case, you found out that the *actual* problem is your friend's fear of being a full-time chauffeur. Now you can proceed to help her solve *that* problem.

Example 4

Your friend says:

"My husband and I aren't getting along. He's up for a promotion, and I really want him to get it. I even give him tips about how he can do it. I thought that by helping him to get the promotion, it would bring us closer. But every time I bring it up, he just gets angry and he doesn't talk to me for days."

As you listen to her, your intuition tells you that she may be the source of the problem because she's offering him help that he doesn't want.

So you could ask:

- Could you be contributing to the problem?
- Have you considered the possibility that he wants to figure this out on his own?
- Could it be that he feels he's got it under control and it's your attempt to help him that's making him angry?

When you're adding your observations or thoughts, you want to choose words and questions that are non-judgmental and respectful. Throughout the clarifying process, you want to approach your friend with the attitude that she has the best intentions, and that she's doing the best she can. By addressing a sticky situation in a sensitive way, you're making it possible for her to keep moving in a positive direction.

OK, you've asked a lot of questions...

What if:

Your friend says she still can't really identify what's bothering her? You can:

- Empathize with her discomfort
- Acknowledge the complexity of the problem
- Throw out a couple of possible names for the problem she's facing
- Tell her that you're not giving up and that you can tackle it again tomorrow
- Encourage her to sleep on it and see what comes to mind
- Say "Maybe this has nothing to do with moving (or the speeding ticket, or the chance for promotion)." Sometimes one change or loss brings up other changes or losses
- Ask, "Have you ever had this feeling before?"
- Suggest that she see a professional counselor, who can get at deep-seated issues that are harder to uncover

What if:

You uncover three different problems?

- You can ask her which problem she wants to work on right away, which one is bothering her the most, which one she feels that you would be most helpful with.

What if:

She replies, "You know, I think I just needed to vent." You can:

- Say, "OK, then, I'm glad I could help you get that off your chest."
- Ask, "Do you feel better now that you've blown off some steam?"
- Say, "That's great, but if at some point you want to go further with this, just let me know."

What if:

She doesn't say it but you get the feeling that she's just venting?

- Say, "I wonder if right now you just need to let off some steam?"
- Just say nothing and let her venting session take its course.
- Say, "I'm glad I could listen today. Let me know if you want to talk more about this another time."

If you're still on the fence about the value of clarifying the issues and defining the problem, here's a classic example from the annals of psychotherapy:

John and Sally visit a couples counselor named Michael. They tell Michael that their friends have sent them to him because of their constant bickering. They think that they'd better learn to stop bickering before they lose their friends.

Michael asks John and Sally if they do, indeed, bicker a lot. They affirm that they do. He asks them if that's a problem for them. They both say no, that they rather enjoy bickering, that their feelings aren't hurt by it, and that they love each other dearly.

Michael suggests that the problem they actually have is that their friends are uncomfortable when they bicker. He then coaches them in refraining from bickering in front of their friends. Everyone is happier.

How Do You Know If Clarifying & DefiningWorked?

You can observe her emotions:

- Is she showing a sense of relief?

You can ask:

- "Are we on the right track?"
- "Have we got it?"
- "Have we nailed the problem?"

You can listen for her to say something like:

- "You ask really good questions"
- "It's a relief to get to the real problem here"
- "I don't know if I could have figured this out myself"
- "OK, now that we know what the problem is, what am I going to do?"

If you don't get these responses, then perhaps it hasn't worked.

If it hasn't worked, you can help by saying:

- "Let's get back together tomorrow and see if we can get to the bottom of this" or

- "I think we've gone as far as we can go to identify the problem. Maybe it would help to bring in someone who knows more about the kind of problem you may be facing. That might be a professional counselor or it might be an accountant, an attorney, or a physician…

If Clarifying the Issues & Identifying the Problem has worked, and you want to go further, you can help by…. **Setting The Goal**

Chapter Four

Setting The Goal

Setting The Goal

In the chapter about listening, we talked about gaining an understanding of your friend's distress. In the chapter on clarifying the issues, we talked about getting to the nature of the problem that is causing his distress, part of which may stem from not having a clear goal. In this chapter, we want to come to an understanding of what his goal will be so he can move from problem to solution.

What Is Setting The Goal?

In the most basic terms, a friend with a problem is telling you, "I don't have what I want." Setting the goal is a way of defining what he wants. It's also a process of making sure the goal is appropriate for him, is within his capabilities, and will lead to a solution of his problem.

- Appropriate means it reflects his personality and his desires.
- Within his capabilities means that he can realistically achieve it.
- Solution-focused means that it will get him what he wants.

In some cases, the goal seems obvious, as in the case of someone who wants to lose twenty pounds. That doesn't mean that you don't want to explore the idea of goals more thoroughly. Perhaps losing twenty pounds is not an appropriate goal for your friend. Or, it may not be within his capabilities to do now. And maybe losing twenty pounds would not solve the problem that he's facing. So, despite what seems like an obvious goal at the outset, your friend may benefit from exploring alternative goals.

In other cases, your friend has no idea what goal he'd like to pursue in order to solve his problem. The problem is all he can see. He can't imagine a way out of the problem, and hasn't been able to think about how he'd like things to be. Here, it becomes particularly important to explore alternative goals, so that for the first time, he can envision a way to solve his problem.

For many problems, there can be a number of potential goals. As the helper, you want to aid your friend to consider possible goals and get to one that's right for him. That means thinking through a list of potential goals to choose the one that your friend can reach, and to assure that it will solve the problem. It may mean discussing, envisioning and finally choosing an alternative.

The goal that he chooses should be one that fits his personality, matches his abilities and will be effective for him. He must feel comfortable enough with the goal that he'll work hard to reach it. You'll know you're on the right track if he says, "I can see going for that." or "If I got there, I would be happy."

Why Does Setting The Goal Help?

Sometimes, when we're in the thick of a problem, our sense of being in control goes out the window.

The power of choosing a goal is that it restores the sense of control.

By helping your friend establish a goal and go from thinking, "I don't know what I want", to "I know what I want," you're helping him regain control and make positive choices about his life.

Setting the goal helps launch your friend into the solution phase. Having listened well, asked questions and defined the issues, you've prepared him to move to the next step, from past difficulty into future resolution.

Up till now, you've heard your friend describe his pain and, perhaps, confusion. You've heard him reveal his weaknesses and vulnerabilities. Maybe he's said, "I can only see one alternative," or "I can only see two paths to take, and they're both extreme," or "I don't know any way I can go from here." Setting the goal helps him re-connect with his own capabilities, power and strength. It helps him see that there may be a number of possible ways to go, and that one of them will be right for him.

Setting the goal helps him move away from feeling stuck in the problem and toward feeling engaged in creating a solution. Feeling stuck is frustrating, anxiety-provoking, demoralizing and exhausting. Feeling stuck may mean feeling isolated, unproductive, unlovable. Contemplating action is the antidote to the feelings generated by being stuck.

Another way setting the goal works is in stimulating positive, future-oriented thinking: it generates hope. Hopelessness changes to hopefulness as he moves from thinking, "There's no end in sight." to "I can see a way out. I don't have to be Superman to get out of this mess. I will be able to get what I want."

Setting the goal

In the thick of a problem, people lose their sense of being in control. You can think of setting the goal as a way to restore that sense of control.

How To Do It

You help your friend set a goal by asking: "What do you want?" Then you help him define it in a clear and tangible way.

Example 1:

"What do you want?"

"I want to lose weight."

"How much weight do you want to lose?"

"Ten pounds."

"By when do you want to lose weight?"

"By New Year's."

This goal would be realistic if your friend is 20 pounds overweight and it's February. It's less realistic if he's 20 pounds overweight and it's November, in which case a more realistic goal would be to lose five pounds (or to change the desired date to March).

Example 2

At a family gathering, your 13 year old nephew Scott comes to you and says: "Somebody is bullying me in the cafeteria every day at lunchtime. I don't like it. What do you think I can do?"

"Do you want to fight back?"

"No, I'm too small."

"Do you want to use humor to deflect the bullying?"

"No, I'm not very good with humor."

"Do you want to avoid the bully?"

"No, I don't think I can always avoid him."

"Do you want to get help from other people?"

"Yes, I want to get some help."

"OK, there's your goal!"

In this example, you helped to supply the ideas for Scott to consider, because he didn't yet have the experience to know what the possible goals might be.

Now Scott has identified a workable goal that he feels positive about. You can ask him to check back with you and let you know if it works. If it doesn't work, you can offer to help him consider other alternatives.

Now that you've read this example and have some idea of what's involved in exploring alternatives, you're either saying to yourself "Now we're getting to the fun part" or "I liked the listening part, but this kind of conversation is not my cup of tea." So, if this is not for you, you can decide not to be the helper. You can refer your friend to a professional helper (see Chapter 8) or leave the helping role (see Chapter 9).

Example 3

Later that evening you're talking to your friend Charles, who tells you that his boss is a bully and he doesn't know what to do.

"What do you want to have happen?"

"I want him to stop yelling at me in staff meetings."

"OK, what could you do?"

"I could stand up to him in the meeting, but that might just make him angrier. I could send him an email before the meeting, but he'd just make fun of me. I could go to HR, but he would just deny that he was bullying me. But maybe I could sit down with him at a quiet time and tell him why his behavior bothers me. If that doesn't work, I could look for another job."

"Great, now you have a goal, and a back-up goal, too."

Setting the goal starts with "What do you want?" and ends with "I know what I want."

How Do You Know If Setting The Goal Has Worked?

If your friend says, "I know what I want and I know how I'm going to get it." This doesn't mean that he'll automatically be successful, but he's motivated to give it a try.

If he says, "I know what I want" and asks, "Can you help me make a plan?" He's motivated and ready, but wants help translating motivation into action. Chapter Six is about helping a friend to make a plan.

If he tells you he want to think about it. He's actually considering the solution that you discussed. He's already farther along than before you had the conversation.

And if Setting the Goal doesn't work, you can help by....

Confronting

Chapter Five

Confronting

Confronting

Here you are, at Chapter Five. You've listened, clarified the issues, defined the problem and set the goal. But what if you still have the feeling that:

- Something is missing
- Something doesn't add up
- Something doesn't ring true
- There's more here than meets the eye

It's time for a reality check.

You have to ask yourself two questions:

1. Is your friend being honest with herself about her role in the problem and her commitment to actually do something about it?

And

2. Is your friend being honest with you in describing the nature of the problem or her commitment to solving it?

Honesty is essential to the process of trying to help. In this context, it means that your friend is willing to examine her role in or contribution to the problem and to discuss it with you. If you feel that she's not being honest, then your role is to confront her.

The friend who says she's "just venting" is a perfect example of the need for confrontation.

Example 1

What if she says she's just "blowing off steam," but you think there's something more going on? In that case, you have to be honest with her and say: "I think this is about more than just blowing off steam."

Example 2

What if a friend describes a problem that she wants to solve, but you think that she's just venting? You have to be able to say "I think you're just blowing off steam," or just let her do so.

What Is Confrontation?

Confronting is pointing out an inconsistency, a mixed message or an omission. It's pointing out an alternative view, another way of looking at the situation.

In one case, this might mean telling your friend that what she's been doing to solve the problem is only making it worse. In another case, it might mean telling her that she - not her partner, boss or neighbor - is the cause of the problem. In a third case, it might mean telling her that there's something that she's not telling you. In a fourth case, it might mean telling her that the problem is beyond her power to solve.

If you ask people whether or not they enjoy confrontation, most people will say "no." They may associate confrontation with raised voices, angry words and hard feelings. They confuse confrontation with arguing.

Confrontation is different than arguing. What's the difference? In an argument, you're trying to show a friend that she's wrong, and win her over to your point of view. That's likely to put her on the defensive, which will increase the tension for both of you.

In confrontation, you're trying to show her that there's another way to interpret the situation she's told you about. You're not trying to prove a point; you're trying to move her past a barrier that's been in her way all along. Your confrontation may provide the breakthrough that finally allows her to consider fresh possibilities for solving her problem.

Think of confrontation as a reality check. The following are examples of confrontation in a helping situation:

- "Have you ever considered that the reason you get so many speeding tickets is that you drive too fast?"
- "Do you think that you're so often disappointed by your employees because your standards for them are unrealistic?"
- "Could the reason that you and your partner argue so much be that neither one of you is willing to talk about an issue before it becomes a problem?"

As you can see, each of these questions is pretty easy to pose without being accusative or causing hurt feelings. They simply sum up a concern that you've had while listening, and put the issue on the table for discussion.

In fact, you'll be surprised how relieved and grateful your friend is when you've cared enough to say what no one else has dared to say.

The Risks of Confrontation

There are two risks that your friend takes when she asks for help. The first is in revealing herself and her vulnerability. She's saying, "I have a problem". Her fear may be that she'll be made to feel bad or wrong, or look like a fool, or get "zapped" in response.

The second risk is in trying to do something different, to change her approach. The process of change is often uncomfortable in and of itself. In addition, your friend may fear that she can't do something different, or, if she did, that she could end up in the same place she started from, or that things could go worse for her rather than better. People will often stick with the approach that they're already taking because "the devil you know is better than the devil you don't."

In our experience, the first risk - that of asking for help and revealing vulnerability - is the more difficult. If you are reading this chapter, it's because your friend hasn't yet taken this risk. With successful confrontation, you can help her achieve this difficult first step.

Once she has fully acknowledged her problem, she'll have the confidence to take the second risk: to make a change and work toward a solution. She may decide not to take those steps just yet, but at least she has a realistic sense of the problem she's facing.

Your friend is not the only one taking a risk. How about the risks you take when you confront her? As we mentioned, no one really likes confrontation. So, if you're deciding whether to confront your friend, you may want to ask yourself:

- Is this relationship strong enough to withstand this process?
- Do you want the drama or the stress of confrontation?
- Do you have any physical or emotional fears about confronting this individual?

If you determine that it's not safe to confront your friend, you may want to say something like:

"You know, we've explored some alternatives, but we don't seem to be getting anywhere. Maybe that's as far as we can go with it. Maybe we should take a break or perhaps you should talk with someone who would be better at helping you."

Why Does Confrontation Help?

Confronting helps because it presents a way to end the cycle of denial and evasion and set the stage for real change to occur. That is, it helps because it enables your friend to see where she's blocking her own progress, and it allows her to get out of her own way.

People resist change, and it's easy to explain why they do. They're already doing what they think is right. They're trying, through their thinking and their behavior, to succeed in life and to avoid failure. They're looking for confirmation and reinforcement that they're on the right track; they're not looking to be told that they're headed in the wrong direction.

You're the one to help your friend view the situation through a different lens. Because you've listened and allowed her to talk without being judged, she may have revealed more to you about the problem than she's ever told anyone before. Your confrontation will work because you can supply a piece of the puzzle that no one knew was missing.

But what if you need to confront her about something that lots of people have pointed out before? Your confrontation will work because she'll be ready to hear from you what she's been unwilling or unable to hear from others.

Confrontation can work because:

If what she's been doing to solve the problem is only making it worse, *you're pointing that out so that she can try something more productive.*

If she's the source of the problem (and not her partner, boss or neighbor), *you're showing her that she holds the key to the solution.*

If there's something she's not telling you, *you're making sure that all the cards are on the table so the problem can be worked on* .

If the problem is beyond her power to solve, *you're helping her to let it go or live with it.*

If she's just venting, *you're not wasting energy working on a solution.*

If she says she's venting but there's more to it, *you're helping her solve the problem by naming it.*

In each case, *you're clearing the path for something to happen that wouldn't have happened if you didn't confront her.*

How To Do It

You do it with confidence. You point out an inconsistency or a mixed message or something that she's left out. You do so in order to enable her to move on. You wouldn't be fulfilling your role as a helper if you didn't point out what's getting in the way. In order for her to solve her problem, you have to help her get it out of the way. So don't be wishy-washy, or worry about hurting her feelings, or be concerned that you're spoiling what you've done so far.

The first step is to describe your own observations. You can say something like:

"Is it OK if I make an observation?"

or

"I think I see something that might be getting in the way."

or

"Based on what you've told me, I come to a different conclusion about the problem. I think it's possible that you've missed the point because, to me, something doesn't add up."

or

"It continues to surprise me that you say 'I want to get in shape' and yet you say 'I'm not giving up beer.'"

or

"I think I see where we're stuck."

or

"I'm thinking that you're missing the role that your behavior is having in all this."

or

"It sounds like you're not the problem here; your partner is an alcoholic."

There are two approaches to confrontation: direct and indirect. How do you decide which one to use? It depends on relationship, temperament and timing.

If your relationship is a long one and you both tend to be pretty candid with each other, you might be direct and say:

"Sounds like you're being stubborn about your son's quitting the football team."

But, if your relationship is more recent, or you tend to be more diplomatic, or if she tends to be more sensitive, then you might say:

"Have you ever considered that being in the school play might be as good a way to prepare for life as being on the football team?"

And sometimes you just go on intuition in deciding whether to be direct or indirect. You might think, regardless of all the other factors, that it makes sense to be as direct as possible in this particular case. Or, you may feel that this issue seems pretty difficult for this person to wrestle with, so you might approach it more cautiously.

Most situations that require confrontation fall into one or more of these four categories.

1. She's been going about it all wrong.

Example

Your friend, a former sales manager, has bought a small restaurant and has told you that morale is low and turnover is high. She says her method of motivating people is to create a competitive environment in which results get rewarded, but that her restaurant employees are lazier than her sales teams ever were. You might say:

"It sounds to me like a competitive environment doesn't work in your business. Maybe restaurant employees want a more cooperative environment and they'd be more motivated to stick around longer if you encourage them to work together, not against each other."

2. She- not her partner, boss or neighbor- is the cause of the problem.

Example

Remember the friend who told you that her husband was having a problem at work? She said it's affecting their relationship and he won't talk to her about it. She tells you that she's asked him a thousand times and the more she asks, the more resistance he gives. You might say:

"Have you ever considered that, from his point of view, you're being intrusive? Perhaps all these questions are just driving him away."

3. She's not telling you something.

Example

Your friend has been on a diet for months, but she's not losing any weight. She tells you that she's careful about her diet all week long and scrupulous about getting exercise every day. You might say:

"If you're following a diet, and still not losing weight, there must be something you're not telling me."

4. She's got a problem that's beyond her power to solve.

Example

Your friend has been diagnosed with bipolar disorder. She tells you that if she uses better self-control, she won't need medication.

"Everything I've read says that self-control is not the problem in bipolar disorder. Even people with great self-control need medication."

Your basic observation, plainly stated, can make all the difference in the world.

How Do You Know If Confronting Worked?

It's worked if she comes right out and says:

"Wow! I guess you're right about that."

or

"Yeah, I guess I have to take responsibility for my part in this problem with my partner."

or

"Thanks; I wish someone had told me that five years ago."

When she can verbalize this kind of response, you know your confrontation has worked. Now you and she can get back to the helping process with information you need to move forward.

How you use the information you uncovered depends on where you were in the process before you staged the confrontation. You may have to go all the way back to listening. Or you may be at the stage of clarifying the issue. Or, you might only have to return to setting the goal and to go on from there toward making a plan, now that she's owned up to what's really going on.

It's worked if you see or hear an emotional response:

- Anger
- Tears
- Laughter
- Shock

When her response is emotional, you have to hit the pause button and slow down. You'll need to address her emotion before going on. You can ask what it is she's feeling and how it relates to the problem:

> "Tell me where the anger's coming from."

> "What I've said seems to have brought on some sadness."

> "Should we talk later about this?"

Or, maybe you just sit with her and wait for her to tell you what she's feeling and thinking.

Once she can verbalize her responses, you can either circle back to listening or clarifying the issue. Or, if she's ready, you can get right into exploring alternatives and making a plan.

What if she gets so angry that she just walks away?

This doesn't mean that you've failed. Sometimes it takes a while for things to sink in. We've all had the experience of realizing only later that someone we thought was way off base was actually right.

If your friend walks away it isn't necessarily a rejection of what you've said. She may need to let her emotions subside. Once they have, she may be able to reconsider your observation and see it in a positive light. She may come back to you at some point to take up where she left off.

It's also worked if, at a later time and with another person, she addresses the ideas you've talked about. You may never know that this has occurred, but you'll have planted the seed that allows this to happen.

Assuming that confrontation has worked, you can help by re-visiting any prior steps that need to be redone and then move on to...

Making A Plan

Chapter Six

Making A Plan

Making A Plan

Helping and planning aren't the same thing.

Planning is part of helping; but it's rarely, if ever, the first part. Any plan that is not preceded by listening, clarifying the issues, defining the problem, and setting a goal is not much more than a well-meaning but ineffective exercise. But you've taken all those preparatory steps, so now you're ready to help your friend make a plan.

What Is Making A Plan?

A plan is a course of action custom-designed to resolve an identified problem. There is no such thing as a ready-made plan that you can select and deliver. Instead, making a plan means helping your friend create the steps it will take to address his specific problem and resolve it to his satisfaction.

His plan might include a number of steps and it could involve a number of people. The plan is for your friend, and it may or may not include you.

For example, your friend may want to get a new job. This may mean doing some research about the industry he's interested in, finding a writer to update his resume, doing some informational interviews to learn more about the occupation that interests him, and so forth.

A process like this may take weeks or months. He'll need a well-thought-out plan to help him stay on track until he finds his next job.

As we mentioned in the chapter on setting the goal, the plan has to be realistic for the person you're helping. You're going to bring to this process your knowledge of him from working, or living, or having lunch with him. A plan that worked for your brother-in-law won't necessarily work for your friend.

You'll know that your friend Bob is shy, but that finding a job requires networking with others. The plan for Bob, then, will have to include strategies for reaching out to others while staying within his comfort zone.

Bob has no concerns, however, about revising his resume. You know that writing comes easily to him. Bob's organized, too, and he's kept his resume up to date over the years. The plan that you and he construct will emphasize activities that get him out in front of people. It won't have to say much about writing his resume.

At this point, we should mention that many people think a plan must be in writing: no ifs, ands or buts. You know us well enough by now to know that we don't believe that there's one size that fits all. It's worth bringing up the question of a written plan. You and your friend can decide whether putting his plan into writing is a good idea.

Written plan or not, the more thought you put into planning, the more effective you'll be in helping.

Why Does Making A Plan Help?

It helps because it's the antidote to the curse of the New Year's resolution. Making a plan links today's thinking with tomorrow's action. You know what we mean. Millions of people first consider their New Year's resolutions at 11:59 PM on December 31st. This year's resolutions may be the same as last year's: "I'm going to get a new job. I'm going to lose 20 pounds. I'm going to get organized."

Why don't these resolutions ever work? Because the person making the resolution never made a plan, or considered what steps to take first, which people to contact, or how to stay on track.

Up to this point your talks with your friend have helped him recognize what's not working for him and what he intends to do instead. He now knows what he wants. By helping him strategize about how to get it, you'll help him connect what he wants to have with what he will do to get there. In planning, he'll feel closer to his goal than just talking about it.

The process of planning moves him from open-ended exploration into concrete activity. While exploration was critical to your friend's understanding of what he wanted to do, taking action can be more satisfying and fulfilling. It can help him regain a feeling of control over his personal or professional life. He'll feel closer to his goal, in planning, than when just talking about it.

A list of wishes is no closer to a plan than a list of words is to a hit song. If he could have found a new job and lost twenty pounds without making a plan, he would have already done so. But now you're moving from conceptual to concrete, from thinking to action, from the big picture to specific steps. By making a plan, your friend will have a much greater chance of success because he'll know what he's going to do, when he's going to do it, and how he's going to do it.

Planning makes the resolution of his problem more real than theoretical and helps him begin to sense the relief that comes with moving in a positive direction.

How To Do It

Some people take an overly optimistic approach to planning. Others are overly pessimistic. Your goal is to steer your friend away from either extreme and help him create a plan that's realistic. A realistic plan is more likely to be followed and more likely to result in success.

Let's use the example of networking, an essential part of career change, to illustrate the issue of optimistic, pessimistic and realistic approaches to planning.

The overly optimistic planner says:

> "I know someone who knows someone at Company X. I'm going to call him and he'll get me in to see the hiring manager right away."

The overly pessimistic planner says:

> "I'll have to make a hundred calls before I even get to talk to somebody."

The realistic planner would say:

> "I'll call the alumni office at my school and get a list of other alums who would be open to networking with me."

Example

Here's an example of a realistic plan for a friend seeking a job. It would probably involve the following steps. He would:

1. Research which organizations he could possibly work for
2. Identify the job titles that those companies give to the positions that he wants

3. Take a look at online and other job postings to see who's hiring these days
4. Reach out to people in his network to see who can help him approach these organizations
5. Write, or have someone help him write, a resume that demonstrates how he can do the job that's being advertised
6. Decide on, and practice, an interviewing strategy
7. Devise and practice a negotiating strategy

Remember: it's his plan, not yours! You're facilitating him in designing the plan. As in listening to help, it's all about him.

Obviously, in setting out a plan like this, you as the helper know that you won't be carrying it out. But you want to make sure that it's a plan that your friend *could* carry out successfully.

Roadblocks are inevitable

The more specific his plan, the more you can help your friend prevent or avoid roadblocks and minimize the risk of setbacks and surprises. The fewer surprises he encounters ("What? I need a resume?!), the more confidence he'll retain and the more energy he'll have for continuing to pursue his objectives.

Every good plan requires a timeline

What comes first, second and third? A timeline is essential to coordinate activities that should help him reach his goal. In carrying out a plan, it's often essential to know how long a given process will take. It will help your friend maintain realistic expectations.

It takes twenty years to be an overnight success unless you're in a real hurry - then it takes twenty-five.

Like any good plan, a timeline can be modified if you find that things go worse than expected (or better).

Markers of success are important along the way. It may take a long time for your friend to find his next job, but every forward step along the way takes him closer to that goal. In his plan, you want to create some milestones on his road to success: to keep him on track, to keep his momentum going, to keep him satisfied that he's on his way to his ultimate goal.

In a job search, he can commemorate:

- Getting his resume ready for his first informational interview

- Printing professional quality copies of his resume
- Making his first appointment
- Completing his first informational interview
- Etc., etc.

These landmarks often seem trivial, but maintaining awareness of them helps him stay positive and committed to his plan. By observing milestones, he can prevent anxiety and doubt from building up.

The process of making a plan is obviously helpful when you want to find a job and be able to pay the bills. Planning is no less important, but often overlooked, in other areas of life such us finding a partner or improving one's health.

How does a person find a partner? The rules of thumb vary from situation to situation. If you don't know what they are, you can look for them in how-to books, you can consult the Internet, you can ask someone for suggestions, and you can draw ideas from movies or songs.

Some general rules of thumb for finding a partner:

1. He'll only meet someone if he gets out of the house. He should choose an activity he enjoys already, and get out there and do it.

But

2. He should choose an activity that the person he's seeking is likely to enjoy also (if he's looking for an athletic female partner, then joining a co-ed softball league would be a good way to find one).

3. The principle of connection: As in job-seeking, the first person he meets may not be the right one, but may be the eventual connection to the person who is right for him. By making a number of connections, he's on his way to his goal, but the first, or even tenth, person he meets may not yet be the one (and sometimes he'll learn, after his tenth connection, that the first person he met was actually the right one for him!). It's important to advise him not to be discouraged, but encouraged, as this process gets under way.

4. The principle of reciprocity: Your friend may meet someone who seems right to him for all the reasons he's listed. But if that person doesn't feel the same attraction, or if she's not ready to be in a relationship at that time, he can't single-handedly make a relationship work. It takes two.

Now, in helping your friend put together his own plan, you can build on these general rules of thumb, but you have to help him make a plan that will work for him. What does he like to do? When does he like to do it? How's his energy level and his available time? What situations make him most comfortable or uncomfortable, and how far is he willing to stretch in pursuit of this goal?

At some point, you'll find that most plans are simple to construct, but they're not easy to follow. You have to remind him of this and advise him to keep a sense of humor and sense of perspective.

You may have no plans to become a career counselor, matchmaker or personal trainer, but you can help a friend plan to get the job he needs, find the partner he wants, or become the regular exerciser he'd like to be.

Though they change over time, there will always be timely Rules of Thumb

---

Before finalizing the plan, you and he should talk about your role, if any, in carrying it out. Your role could be as structured as participating with your friend in some of the tasks that he's doing

How Can I Help?

(such as exercising regularly), or providing a regular phone call to check in on him. Your role could be a less defined one, though, of just being available on an as-needed basis to talk about how things are going.

In the discussion about the role you'll play, you want to bring out the possibility that things may not go according to the plan that you've helped him put together. At that point, then, your role is to help him re-evaluate, refine or re-create his plan.

It's always tempting to give advice, but it rarely works, for a variety of reasons:

- *It may be inappropriate*
- *It can be ill-timed*
- *It could be unrelated to the issue*

You'll know that you've fallen into advice-giving when your friend says, "Yes, but...". If you're making a plan, he'll say, "Yes, and...". When he feels that he's come up with his own solution, he's more likely to get started and to have the motivation to follow through when difficulties occur, as they inevitably will.

How Do You Know If Making A Plan Has Worked?

You'll know it's worked if you get a job announcement, a wedding announcement, or a photo of your friend finishing a 5k.

You'll know it's worked if he's started his plan and is actively taking the steps toward achieving his goal.

You'll also know that it's working if he returns to talk with you about *slightly changing* the plan to make it more effective. This demonstrates that he's put enough time into the original plan to know where it's helpful and where it falls short.

If, after making the plan, your friend gets bogged down and loses his momentum, you can help by…

Keeping On Track

Chapter Seven

Keeping On Track

Keeping On Track

"If anything can go wrong, it will."

Murphy's Law

We know, we know, we know. As you read the last chapter, many of you were thinking, "We've listened, we've clarified, we've set the goal, we've confronted, and we've made a plan. That's it, end of story, that's how you help."

The rest of you may have been around the block enough times to know that no matter how far you go, or how fast you run, you can't out-run Murphy's law.

And so the story continues.

What is Keeping on Track?

Basically, helping your friend stay on track means helping her execute the plan she's devised, in whatever role you have agreed to play.

You might have built into the plan a way for you to stay in the loop. For example, you could be the person to whom your friend reports. This could be a formal weekly report, conducted over coffee every Saturday afternoon or lunch on Thursday. It could be a weekly e-mail that you expect to get every Friday morning. It's a common practice for coaches or counselors to schedule a weekly telephone call to talk about progress or any difficulties that arise during the week. If it fits the nature of your relationship, you could schedule a weekly phone call with your friend.

There are of course plenty of ways to keep in touch informally. You and your friend may agree that she'll be in touch with you as needed. It may be to tell you about her successes, or to ask for some help with some difficulties. Depending on her style and yours, she might ask to meet in person, give you a phone call, or send an e-mail.

You could have a shared understanding that you're available to talk if she wants to talk. It's up to you to decide whether to contact her if you haven't heard from her for a while. If you know her pretty well, you may have an intuition about when she needs a little help. We've all had the experience of calling a friend and having them say, "I was just thinking of calling you." So, trust your intuition and make the call or send the e-mail.

Maybe your original role in her plan is more hands-on than just staying in touch. Perhaps you've agreed to walk with her once a week so that she exercises more. Or you've said you would take care of her kids while she attends an evening class. Or you might have offered to drive her to a job interview that's coming up.

In these more hands-on situations, you'll have more of an opportunity to see how well things are going. You'll know whether she's gone off course and needs some help getting back to doing the things she said she'd do.

Why Does Keeping On Track Help?

To risk stating the obvious, longstanding problems don't arise overnight, and they won't disappear overnight. The plan you've designed to reach the solution she's seeking may require many steps over time, and will probably need support and fine-tuning along the way.

As you listened to your friend, you learned a lot about your friend's strengths and weaknesses as well as the nature of her problem. Therefore, you'll be able to provide the kind of support and type of encouragement she needs to stick with it when the road is long and unexpected roadblocks arise. By keeping her on track through this long process, you're helping to assure that she will, eventually, meet her goal.

You may be the only other person who knows about her problem, the plan that she's working on, and how meaningful even a small step forward is. Her progress may be invisible to the other people in her life, and she might even miss it herself. Or, if others do notice her steps, they may be critical and judgmental about what she's doing.

On top of that, she may be self-critical and pessimistic about her ability to succeed. Catching her doing something right and telling her about it in a positive way will be a powerful reinforcement for her to continue what she's doing. You'll prevent her from falling back into old, counter-productive patterns. The support that you give her is a reminder that you recognize her struggle and believe that she'll ultimately succeed. Even your smallest "Good goin'!" can help her keep up the positive momentum towards her long-term goal.

A Word About Change

A common belief is that, when it comes to change, you're not successful unless you've achieved 100% change. In reality, a change of 15% makes a significant difference. Once you've helped your friend get to 15%, it should be pretty easy to help her recognize how far she's come and decide whether she can and wants to go further.

How To Do It

Remember those milestones that you spent so much time talking about and building into the plan? You can keep her on track by reminding her of these milestones and helping her remain optimistic about her eventual success as she passes each intermediate goal. Identify and talk about any progress that she's made so far and encourage her to keep at it.

You've helped her make a plan that's based on the goals she wants to achieve. You also want to keep her focused on those goals and the way the plan she's following will help her reach them.

Everybody's different. Some may be helped to stay on track by being reminded to give themselves small rewards as they pass each milestone. You can ask directly: "Did you take the rest of the afternoon off after finishing your resume?" or "Did you buy the book you wanted after you lost that first five pounds?"

Some people may not need the time off or the new book to read in order to stay with their plan. But almost everyone responds to an acknowledgement that they have reached that interim milestone that they are making progress.

Catch your friend doing something right, small as it may be, whenever you can. When the ultimate goal is still far off, your acknowledgement will mean a lot to her. It will remind her to recognize the small steps she's already made, and not take them for granted.

One of the most significant things that professional counselors do is point out these small successes to clients. By pointing out these small successes and praising clients for making those changes in their lives, counselors help clients learn how to become their own cheering section. You'll be doing this as well when you identify and praise your friend's small steps as she takes them.

It's not always a straight path to the goal line. Your friend may have zigged when she should have zagged. Your job is to remind her that missteps are bound to happen and that it's natural to feel discouraged from time to time. She's still up and running; the game's not over.

Your friend might feel that she should have solved the problem by now, that if she doesn't get to her goal soon enough, it will be too late. Here's your chance to say something very corny. "Patience," you can say, "is a virtue." Reminding her of the relationship between her plan and her goal can help her see that every step has a purpose. She might be tempted to take a shortcut by skipping a step, but that would be counter-productive.

When things aren't going according to plan, people tend to judge themselves or expect others to judge them, and that's not a productive use of time. If you don't want your friend to waste time and energy getting stuck in a cycle of judgment, tell her that missteps are a natural part of the process, not a character flaw. Her time will be much better spent in re-grouping and getting back on track.

How Do You Know
If Keeping On Track Worked?

You know that helping someone stay on track has
worked if:

- She regains her momentum after a setback,
  and picks up where she left off.
- She asks your help in re-strategizing or fine-
  tuning her plan.
- She says that you helped her prepare for the
  roadblock that she's actually encountered.
  She may ask for your help to get around it,
  or tell you that she's already done so!

And if keeping her on track doesn't work, you
can help by...

Finding A Professional Helper

Chapter Eight

Finding
Professional Helpers

Finding
Professional Helpers

For many of you, this may be the first chapter you turn to. Your friend has a problem and you know it's beyond your ability to help, or that it's within your ability but beyond your desire. Or maybe you've already spent quite a bit of time trying to help a friend and are frustrated that he's unable to make the kind of progress you thought he could make with your help.

What is Finding a Professional Helper?

Helping someone find a professional helper is what you do when you've reached your limit, are frustrated or overwhelmed. If you feel like giving up, you know you're there. Still, you don't want to give up on your friend. At this point, the best way to help is to bring someone else into the picture. The question is "Who ya gonna call?!" That is, who's *he* gonna call?

He calls an attorney if he has a legal problem. He calls an accountant or a financial planner if it's a financial issue. He calls a therapist or a mediator if it's a relationship problem. He calls a career counselor if it's a career issue. He calls an M.D. if it's a health-related problem.

No surprises here. Why, then, would your friend need help in taking a step that seems so obvious? There are two reasons. One is that your friend must admit to himself that his problem is of this magnitude. We'll talk more about that in the next section of this chapter.

The second reason is that when people are feeling vulnerable, they can be reluctant to do something they haven't done before. For anyone who's never done it, the prospect of calling an attorney,

career counselor, financial planner, or psychotherapist might seem intimidating.

If your friend routinely works with legal issues,
he wouldn't think twice about calling an attorney,
but the prospect of picking up the phone to call a
therapist to talk about personal problems is something else altogether.

Calling one helper is no different than calling
another. The trick is knowing what to say. When
your friend calls a plumber, he'd say "I have a
leaky faucet. Can you come out and take a look?"
He would expect that a plumber, who's in the
business of fixing leaky faucets, would welcome
the call and do his best to solve your friend's problem. The formula is the same when he needs to
call other professional helpers: "I have a problem
about X and I want to talk about it." The professional helper will know what to say and what to
do when he or she answers the phone.

So what is "helping them find a professional
helper?" Let's sum up. First, you reach your limit
in helping. Second, you tell your friend that you'd
like to help, but that someone else could be more
effective. Then you brainstorm with him about
what kind of professional help he needs and what
to say when he makes the call.

Why Does Finding A Professional Helper Work?

The short answer to this question is: the professional has more training and experience in helping solve your friend's specific problem than you do.

Example

Suppose your friend is having a problem getting the ants out of his house. When he calls you, he tells you he's tried alcohol, ammonia, bug spray, vinegar, and he's put ant traps all around the foundation of his house. The ants, though, are still there. You listen to his tale of woe and say, "It's time to call in a pro."

This is an example of the kind of practical problem that friends help each other with all the time. You help your friend in this case by reminding him that *there's no more that he can do on his own*. This sounds like a small thing, but you would be surprised how big a difference this can make. He may have lost sight of the option of calling a professional while he was in the midst of trying to solve the problem by himself. Or, he might have been trying to save money. If that's the case, you can remind him that lower-cost help is often out there and that a financial investment may be warranted.

It's the same when you try to help someone dealing with career, emotional, financial, legal, medical, or other problems. There are professionals who have the specific training and experience to analyze, diagnose and help your friend tackle the problem with a more comprehensive solution. A career counselor, psychotherapist, accountant, attorney, or physician may be what he needs right now.

Certain problems are beyond the scope of the well-intentioned friend or colleague that you are. The following are examples of problems beyond the layperson's scope:

- Financial problems
- Medical problems
- Addictions: smoking, substance dependence, gambling, etc.
- Emotional problems that are deeply rooted or severe: depression, anxiety, bipolar disorder, some forms of stress, recklessness or risk-taking
- Behavioral issues: anger management, partner abuse

Often, two or more of these issues overlap. For example, smoking can cause medical problems, which cause financial problems, which lead to depression. A situation this complex and potentially dangerous makes it critical that you find a professional.

Without question, there are problems that require professional help. Calling a professional enables your friend to go beyond the remedies he's tried and get the help he needs to resolve his problem. What's more, it prevents you from getting entangled in a situation that's beyond your ability to handle.

How To Do It

The first step is to say, without judgment, that the issue your friend is dealing with is important enough or painful enough or complex enough that it warrants professional help.

You can say that you see no benefit in suffering. He can find someone out there who will help him move through his difficulty better or faster than you alone can.

You might be worried that he'll think you're just trying to get rid of him. In fact, the opposite is true. He's more likely to feel that you understand, recognize the seriousness of his problem, and care enough to say it out loud.

In fact, you can further demonstrate your real concern and regard by telling him that you'll assist him in finding that professional help.

Many people have never had to search for professional helpers, and don't know how to do it. They don't know how to find the right person, they don't know what to say, and they don't know what to expect.

Here are some rules of thumb for you and your friend:

1. Get a referral

Example

Suppose your friend needs to have a will drawn up. If you open the phonebook or look online, you may see listings for hundreds of attorneys. How do you know whom he should call? Here are a few ideas:

- Ask another friend if he's ever made a will, and, if so, if he liked the attorney he worked with.
- Ask your accountant if she knows an attorney that she'd recommend.
- Call the local Bar Association and ask for a directory of estate planning attorneys.

- Call a community service group such as a small business association.
- Contact a local law school and ask about graduates who work in this field.

2. Interview the professional you've identified.

Example

Suppose your friend needs a professional psychotherapist. This is a field in which "personal chemistry" can mean a lot. Just because a person has the right professional training doesn't mean that she'd be the right therapist for your friend. In order to find someone with whom he could speak openly and honestly, and have confidence in their ability to help, he could:

- Call the therapist's office and listen to her outgoing message to see whether it sounds like someone he could talk to
- Speak with the therapist on the phone to see whether she's easy to talk to
- Make an appointment and observe his comfort level with the therapist and his confidence about the therapist's ability to help him

It might take your friend a couple of sessions with a psychotherapist before he is sure about his confidence in this professional, and that's OK.

3. Discuss his experience with the professional helper as needed.

You can offer to talk with him about his experience in finding a professional helper by asking questions like:

- "Was he easy to talk to?"
- "Was he a good listener?"
- "Did he understand your problem?"
- "Are you confident that he can help you?"

A word about confidentiality

Keep in mind that psychotherapy and other professional helping relationships do involve confidentiality. Assure your friend that he can talk with you about his experience without discussing the content of his conversation with the professional counselor.

Reminder: Change happens when people step outside their comfort zones. You may have to go outside your own comfort zone when speaking with your friend about the need to call in a professional, especially if his issues are personal or private. Now he needs to go outside his comfort zone to get the help he needs in solving his problem.

How Do You Know If Finding A Professional Worked?

It's worked if he tells you that:

- He found a helper
- He made an appointment
- He kept the appointment
- He's going back to meet with the professional helper again
- He's solved the problem, with the helper's guidance

These are the clues that tell you whether or not he's found that professional helper and is engaged in, or has completed, the process. He may *tell* you that he's having success, or that it's working. Or you may *see* that it's working: he's looking happier, he's accepted a new job, he's quit drinking.

If this hasn't worked...

You may have to set a limit to avoid being pulled back in as the helper or made to feel guilty about turning him over to the professional helper. Having determined that he needs professional counseling, it would be a waste of your time and energy - and his - to do anything less.

To avoid a dialogue that's an endless loop-

Finding Professional Helpers

"You need professional help."

"No I don't."

"Yes, you do."

It's best to simply tell your friend "I can't talk with you about this until you find professional help." Your setting that limit is the *best* way you can help him resolve his problem.

Whether or not you successfully refer your friend to a professional helper, the next and final step is...

Leaving The Helping Role

137

Chapter Nine

Leaving The Helping Role

Leaving The Helping Role

There will come a day when you've completed your role as helper. This may be a role that you came to enjoy, even if you had some fears about it when you started. If you followed the advice we've given, you probably did a pretty good job.

Throughout the helping process you've been disciplined about keeping the focus on your friend. By maintaining this one-sided relationship, you allowed her to gain understanding and do the things she needed to resolve her problem.

It's important, though, to return to the two-way relationship that you had before. You want to avoid the potential risk of your temporary role morphing into a permanent one.

You might think that going back to your former role would be as easy as spreading butter on toast. But we've heard people describe it as being more like trying to get butter off toast.

We wouldn't be surprised if some of you have had this experience - establishing yourself in the helping role and then finding it hard to get out. You may find it satisfying to be in the helping role, your friends may want you in that role, or it may just have become routine. Hollywood has a term for this; it's called typecasting.

What Is Leaving The Helping Role?

Leaving the helping role is the last step in the process, and it's as important as listening was in the first step. You had to work hard to keep your focus on your friend and what she was saying. Now, in order to close this chapter in your relationship, you have to be conscious about ending the role you've played as helper.

Just as you consciously shift your behavior when you return to work after a long holiday weekend, so you and your friend have to shift your behavior when you return to the relationship you had before the helping process began.

You're putting aside one way of relating and resuming another. You're signifying that the helping is over and you're going back to the rhythm of your old friendship. You're saying, "I'm no longer your helper; I'm your friend." Putting it in the terms we used in the Listening chapter, you won't be listening to help, you'll be in conversational mode.

Why Does Leaving The Helping Role Help?

Leaving the helping role allows your friend to re-establish the rhythm of her life and her work. It can give her back a sense of privacy or autonomy around the issue that you've helped her with. With respect to the problem, it puts the ball back in her court, which is where it belongs at this point. It gives her the choice to bring it up with you again or not, to talk with you about it again or not.

You don't want to get stuck in the role of being the helper or to stick your friend with the role of being "the one with the problem". Nothing kills a good relationship like people locking each other into inflexible roles. Leaving the helper role helps to re-balance the relationship by restoring the two-way, back and forth nature of your conversations rather than preserving the one-way interactions characteristic of the helping process.

You're moving back into the relationship that you wanted or needed to have in the first place. You and your friend enjoy being friends; you and your colleague need to work together; you and your son need to live together as parent and child. Leaving the helping role allows you to get back to the relationship that you originally chose or molded.

Leaving the role has an additional benefit for you as the helper. It removes you from being the go-to person for every problem or setback that your friend encounters. If she has the tendency to career from one problem to another, you don't want to be stuck in the never-ending role of helper, to always be there, available on a moment's notice. Let's face it: you might be the best unpaid therapist your friend has ever had, but it's your life and you have other interests and obligations.

How To Do It

Transitions are always hard to go through. In a transition like this, one or both people may be reluctant to acknowledge that the time has come to put this episode behind you. One of you - in this case *you* - has to say something.

You can do one, or a combination of, the following things:

1. Recognize the work that your friend has put into solving her problem.
2. Review some of her challenges and what she did to overcome them.
3. Express your satisfaction in having been able to help her.
4. Express your confidence that she'll be able to reach her goals.
5. Do something to celebrate the success you both have had.

Example

"Sharon, you've really worked hard at regaining your confidence about getting out there and dating. Remember how you had a hard time picking up the telephone and making that first call? You felt like you had no idea what people talk about on the phone these days. You were unsure what kind of relationship you wanted at this point in your life or how to break off a relationship that didn't work. But you got on the phone and learned how to have those conversations, how to get past the small talk of a first date, and how to evaluate what you really wanted.

I'm glad I could be there with you to offer some suggestions and encourage you. Going through this together has been really satisfying for me, especially when I see how well it's gone for you. I know that you'll be able to keep pushing yourself to get out there and find the person who's right for you. Why don't we celebrate by going to the movies on Wednesday? You don't need my help with the dating issue any more, so it will be nice to go for coffee afterwards and just talk about the film."

We're not suggesting that you write a speech. We can tell you that your friend will probably have something that *she* wants to say. If she says all the things that you were thinking about saying, just reply, "You're welcome. I'm glad I was able to help." If she doesn't, and you think that the issue of moving on is still up in the air, you may want to fill in the points she missed and emphasize that the helping relationship is ending.

If she resists this ending, and says that she needs more of your help, you have a decision to make. You can say, "OK, let's spend a little more time on this before we agree that we're finished." Remember, you don't want to get stuck in the helper role, so make sure you set a time limit.

Or you can say, "I want to go back to our being just friends, so let's think about who else may be able to help". At that point, you'll talk with her about getting a professional helper (see the prior chapter on this topic) so that she can gain the confidence to proceed, and your old relationship can be restored.

A word about obligation

The person you've helped could feel that she's obligated to you for what you've done, that she owes you something, and that she wants to be available to help you in the future. Letting her express her sense of appreciation and obligation is all you need to do. It's enough to say "thank you" and tell her that you'll keep it in mind.

Another word about obligation

You might feel that, having helped, you have an obligation to maintain a friendship, whether you really want to or not. But having helped creates no more future obligation on your part than it does on hers. What happens next is as much up to you as it is to her. Focus now on ending the helping relationship. Over time, you'll discover whether you want the friendship to continue.

How Do You Know If Leaving The Helping Role Worked?

You know that it's worked if you can be together without her problem becoming the main topic of conversation over and over again. Or, if it does come up, it's only to acknowledge that she's continuing to follow her plan. You can spend time together without feeling like you're being pulled back into the helping role and its one-way focus.

You know it's worked when you have more time and energy available to manage the other obligations in your life. As you're sitting at a stoplight, you're thinking about what to do on the weekend, rather than worrying about your friend's problems.

Chapter Ten

Summing Up

Summing Up

Throughout the pages of this book, we've tried to give you some basic guidelines, distilled from years of practice, for helping a friend, colleague or family member overcome a problem.

Here's how *we'll* know it's worked.

If it's helped you to:

1. Know that you can learn to be a better listener, to help someone define a problem, to confront someone who isn't being honest about a problem, etc.
2. Recognize that the decision is yours, to help or not to help, and how far to take the helping process.

3. Be familiar enough with the helping process to make a knowledgeable decision about whether to help or not.
4. Accept that helping can be a complex process over time, or merely a focused hour of good listening. That listening is often the critical factor, and sometimes the only real factor, in helping.
5. Know what to do, why to do it, how to do it, and how to know when it's helped, so that you know what to do next and when to stop.
6. Understand that you are not a therapist, and that many situations require professional help.
7. Feel comfortable about seeking additional resources, and have some ideas about how to find them.
8. Be aware that you can exit the helping process at any step. You can then choose to return to your prior relationship or not.
9. Understand that you really can make a big difference in someone's life, and have the confidence to give it a go.

We hope that you've enjoyed reading this book as much as we've enjoyed writing it together. Most of all, we hope that you find it useful when you have the opportunity to help.

Anna and Joe

Anna Ranieri, PhD, has a private practice in career counseling, psychotherapy, and executive coaching. Anna enjoys helping people navigate the transitions in their lives and pursue their personal and professional goals.

Joe Gurkoff, MA, is an author, consultant, and educator, recognized for his novel, perceptive and sometimes surprising approaches to helping people solve problems in their business and personal lives.

www.ingramcontent.com/pod-product-compliance
Lightning Source LLC
Chambersburg PA
CBHW071052040426
42443CB00013B/3318